SCHOLASTIC

Ready-to-Use
Independent Reading
Management Kit:
Grade 1

by Beverley Jones and Maureen Lodge

D1302327

New York • Toronto • London • Auckland • Sydney
Mexico City • New Delhi • Hong Kong • Buenos Aires

Teaching *Resources*

Dedication

We would like to thank all our first-grade
students, past and present. We continue
to learn and grow through them.

Cover design by Jason Robinson
Cover photograph by Studio 10
Interior design by Ellen Matlach for Boultinghouse & Boultinghouse, Inc.
Cover and interior illustrations by Maxie Chambliss

ISBN: 0-439-49161-4
Copyright © 2005 by Beverley Jones and Maureen Lodge
Published by Scholastic Inc.

3 4 5 6 7 8 9 10   40   13 12 11 10 09 08 07

Contents

Introduction 5
How to Use This Book 6

Fiction 1
Independent Reading Contract 9
Story Beginning 10
    plot
Character Stars 11
    character
Favorite Picture 12
    comprehension
Question and Answer 13
    ending marks
Syllable Sort 14
    syllables
Short-*a* Poster 15
    *short-*a* words*

Fiction 2
Independent Reading Contract 16
Who? What? Where? 17
    comprehension
Main Event 18
    plot
Create a Cover 19
    comprehension
What Did They Say? 20
    quotation marks
Adjective Balloons 21
    adjectives
Barnyard Vowels 22
    *short-*e* and long-*e* words*

Fiction 3
Independent Reading Contract 23
Plot Train 24
    sequence of events
Up, Up, and Away! 25
    character

Picture This! 26
    setting
Word Soup 27
    capitalization of proper nouns
Sight Word Search 28
    sight words
Action! 29
    action verbs

Fiction 4
Independent Reading Contract 30
Library List 31
    character; inference
Favorite Part 32
    plot
Setting Chart 33
    setting; text to world
Treasure Chest 34
    apostrophes; character
ABC Order 35
    alphabetical order
Short-*i* Fish 36
    *short-*i* words*

Fiction 5
Independent Reading Contract 37
Character Chart 38
    character; text to self
Problem Solved! 39
    problem and solution
Book Award 40
    comprehension
Word Boat 41
    contractions
Sentence Scramble 42
    word order
Dog and Bone 43
    *short-*o* and long-*o* words*

Nonfiction 1

Independent Reading Contract 44
Idea Flower 45
main idea and details
Ask the Author. 46
comprehension
Take a Look 47
graphic aids
Great Sentences! 48
sentence types; ending marks
Noun Search 49
nouns
Ducks in a Row 50
short-u words; alphabetical order

Nonfiction 2

Independent Reading Contract 51
Fact Kites 52
comprehension
Be an Explorer! 53
comprehension
Follow the Footprints. 54
sequence of events
What Do You See? 55
series comma
Title Time 56
capitalization of titles
New Words 57
vocabulary

Nonfiction 3

Independent Reading Contract 58
People and Places. 59
comprehension
True or False?. 60
comprehension
Most Interesting Part 61
comprehension
Rainbow Words 62
synonyms

What Do They Do? 63
subject and predicate
Nice Mice. 64
long and short vowels

Nonfiction 4

Independent Reading Contract 65
Time to Retell 66
retelling
In the Picture. 67
captions
Blast Off! 68
description
Alphabet Search. 69
word search
Adjective Chart 70
adjectives and nouns
Word Frogs 71
vocabulary

Nonfiction 5

Independent Reading Contract 72
Send a Postcard 73
comprehension
Butterfly Chart. 74
fact and opinion
Lots of Learning! 75
comprehension
Book Reviews 76
quotation marks
Old Sock, New Sock. 77
antonyms
Super Sentences. 78
verbs and adjectives

Additional Reproducible Forms

Letter Home. 79
Blank Contract. 80

Introduction

Ready-to-Use Independent Reading Management Kit: Grade 1 provides an instant and easy way to manage your independent reading program and help students meet the language arts standards—all year long! The kit includes ten reproducible activity packs—five for fiction and five for nonfiction—that can be used with any book. Designed especially for first graders, the reproducible pages feature easy-to-read directions, appealing illustrations, and a wide variety of reading-response activities that build skills in comprehension, writing, phonics, grammar, vocabulary, punctuation, and more.

Each activity pack begins with an independent reading contract, which shows at a glance all nine activities in that pack. For each contract, students make choices about which reading, writing, and skills activities they will complete. This fosters a sense of responsibility and ownership and motivates children to put forth their best effort. This program helps students learn to select appropriate books, organize the materials they need, and work independently on meaningful and structured activities that help them get the most out of what they read. The program also allows you to work with one group of students while the rest work independently on their contracts.

Each contract includes three categories of activities:

Reading   Students read to themselves and others.

Writing   Students respond in writing to their books.
- Fiction activities reinforce story elements, such as character, plot, setting, and problem and solution.
- Nonfiction activities focus on nonfiction features and structures such as graphic aids, captions, main idea and details, and sequence of events.

Skills   Students complete activities that connect to their independent reading and also reinforce skills in phonics, vocabulary, punctuation, capitalization, and parts of speech.

The variety of activities within each contract and the flexibility to use the contracts with any book will help you meet the needs of all your learners. The section titled "How to Use This Book" on pages 6–8 provides detailed information on using the contracts. We hope that you will find this book to be a valuable resource for managing your independent reading program, enriching reading experiences, and building key skills. Happy reading!

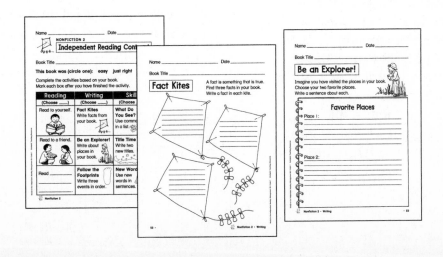

How to Use This Book

Setting Up Your Reading Center

When building your classroom library, choose fiction and nonfiction books that represent a range of reading levels. To help children make selections easily, arrange the books by level in boxes or on shelves, separating fiction and nonfiction. We have found that it is helpful to store the independent reading contracts and copies of the activity pages in our reading center with the books. To help children work independently, show them where everything is kept and where to put away materials when they have finished using them.

Selecting Reading Contracts

Independent reading contracts work with any level of book and are designed for fiction and nonfiction. Choose either a fiction or nonfiction contract, depending on what you would like students to focus on in the next few weeks. In the table of contents, you'll find the titles of the activity pages in each contract, as well as the skills and topics these activities reinforce. You might use the contracts in order from 1 to 5, alternating fiction and nonfiction, or you might choose contracts based on your current areas of study. For example, choose Fiction 3 if you are studying plot sequence or Nonfiction 4 if students are learning about captions.

Preparing Reading Contracts

At the top of each activity column on the contract sheet, you will find a space to fill in the number of activities you would like students to complete. Determine the number based on the amount of time you would like students to spend on the contract, or modify the assignment for individual students. As students become more comfortable with the contracts and are ready for more of a challenge, assign more activities in each column.

The last box of the reading column is open-ended so that you can fill in a reading assignment for students (read to a teacher, read to a family member, and so on). This presents another opportunity to modify the contract for individual students—for example, you might have students read to you or a reading specialist.

We have found that it works best to have all students work on the same contract at the same time. We set aside a two- or three-week period for each contract. During this time, a student may complete a contract for one book, while another student may complete the same contract for three books. It simplifies the process to have students work on the same contract so that you can set up materials and plan mini-lessons geared toward that contract. (Use the template on page 80 to create additional contracts.)

> *Teacher Tip* Independent reading offers a great opportunity to involve family members in students' learning experiences. One way to do this is to write "Read to someone in your family" in the last box of the reading column. It is a good idea to tell families about independent reading contracts at the beginning of the school year. Send home the reproducible letter on page 79 or explain the program at an open house.

Helping Students Select Books

To introduce independent reading contracts in your classroom, begin by demonstrating how to choose a book that is "just right" for the reader. For example, suggest questions for students to ask themselves, such as:

- Can I read most of the words in this book?
- Does the topic of this book interest me?
- Can I read this book without needing much help?

Introducing New Skills

Before introducing an independent reading contract, review the activities and note the skills children need to complete it. For instance, before beginning the Fiction 1 contract, children will need to understand syllables and recognize short-*a* words. One or two weeks before introducing the contract, conduct mini-lessons to introduce these skills. Students will then have the opportunity to practice these skills as they are completing their contracts.

When introducing topics such as adjectives or contractions, you may want to write examples of these words on a poster. Students can then refer to the poster to complete activities that ask them to find examples of these words in their book. That way, if a student's book selection does not include many examples of these types of words, he or she can use the ones from the poster. In our classrooms, students have also enjoyed adding to the posters as they come across "poster words" in their books.

Modeling the Process

Once children have selected their books, model how to use an independent reading contract. Start by reading aloud a book to students. Then make an overhead transparency of either the Fiction 1 or Nonfiction 1 contract sheets. Give each student a photocopy of the contract. After reading the book, show students the contract on the overhead projector. Fill in the name, date, and book title lines and circle the reading level (easy, just right, or hard). Explain that each student will fill in this information and complete the activities based on his or her own independent reading book.

Point out that the first column on a contract lists reading activities. Tell students that they should always begin by completing the first activity in the reading column, which is to read a part of the book to themselves.

Connections to the Language Arts Standards

The activities in this book are designed to support you in meeting the following language arts standards for students in grades K–2 outlined by Mid-continent Research for Education and Learning, an organization that collects and synthesizes national and state K–12 curriculum standards.

—**Uses the general skills and strategies of the reading process**

—**Uses grammatical and mechanical conventions in written compositions**

—**Uses reading skills and strategies to understand and interpret a variety of literary texts**
- Knows setting, main characters, main events, sequence, and problems in stories
- Knows the main ideas of a story
- Relates stories to personal experiences

—**Uses reading skills and strategies to understand and interpret a variety of informational texts**
- Understands the main idea and supporting details of simple expository information
- Summarizes information found in texts
- Relates new information to prior knowledge and experience

Source: *Content Knowledge: A Compendium of Standards and Benchmarks for K–12 Education* (4th ed.) (Mid-continent Research for Education and Learning, 2000)

Next, draw attention to the second box in the reading column, which asks students to read to a friend. With a student, role-play appropriate ways to ask classmates to be reading partners. Demonstrate an appropriate volume for reading aloud. Review the last reading assignment that you have filled in and explain your guidelines for it.

Show students how to make a mark in the corresponding square on their contract when they have finished an activity. (A check mark or X works well.) Point out the number of activities per column that students should complete. Explain that after children have finished the reading activities, they can complete the activities in the other columns in any order. Show students where they can find activity pages and remind them to match the title of the activity on the contract to the title on the activity page. (It is helpful to keep the activity pages for each contract in a labeled folder.) An alternative is to determine which activities students will complete, then staple the corresponding activity pages to the contract in advance.

Once students are comfortable with the procedures, have them work independently while you meet with individuals or small groups. This is also a good opportunity to hold conferences with students who have finished a contract. (See Completing a Contract, at right.)

Starting New Contracts

If a student has finished a contract and if time permits, the student may complete the same contract for a new book. Students can use the same contract for several books because the responses for each book will be different.

When you feel students are ready to move on to new skills, have them progress to the next contract. We have found that students are ready to move on to a new contract about every three weeks. It is a good idea to introduce each new contract, model how to use it, and review procedures as needed.

Storing Work in Progress

Help students organize their materials so that they can work effectively on their own. Have them store all their materials for their current contract, including their book, in a pocket folder. It is helpful for students to staple their contract to the inside left of their folders for easy reference. Designate a place to store the folders, such as in desks, cubbies, or a file-folder box.

Teacher Tip To keep an ongoing record of students' oral reading skills, set up an audio recording station in your classroom. If possible, invite parent volunteers to help students record themselves reading passages from their books throughout the year. Write a short note explaining that you are keeping recordings of students' oral reading throughout the year. Photocopy the note and send it home to families along with their child's audiotape in a resealable plastic bag.

Completing a Contract

Once a student has finished an independent reading contract, he or she is ready to "check out." Have students staple together all their completed activity pages with the contract on top and place this in a designated spot. (This could be a basket on your desk or a file-folder box in a reading center.) Periodically check to see which students have finished their contracts so that you can schedule conferences with them. Conferences offer good opportunities to discuss students' selection of independent reading materials, help them evaluate their work, and assess their comprehension.

Name _____ Date _____

Independent Reading Contract

Book Title _____

This book was (circle one):   easy   just right   hard

Complete the activities based on your book.
Mark each box after you have finished the activity.

Reading	Writing	Skills
(Choose ____)	**(Choose ____)**	**(Choose ____)**
Read to yourself.	**Story Beginning** Draw a picture and write about it.	**Question and Answer** Write a question and answer it.
Read to a friend.	**Character Stars** Name the characters.	**Syllable Sort** Find words with one or two syllables.
Read _____ _____ _____ .	**Favorite Picture** Write about a picture.	**Short-*a* Poster** Find short-*a* words. cat nap

Name _____ Date _____

Book Title _____

Story Beginning

How did the story start?
Draw a picture of the beginning.
Write a sentence about it.

_____

- -

_____

- -

_____

Ready-to-Use Independent Reading Management Kit: Grade 1   Scholastic Teaching Resources

☆ **Fiction I • Writing**

Name _____ Date _____

Book Title _____

Character Stars

Who are the characters
in your book?
Draw the main character
in the big star.
Draw other characters
in the small stars.
Write their names.

Name _____ Date _____

Book Title _____

Favorite Picture

Find your favorite picture.
Write the page number:

_____
....
_____

What do you see in the picture?

_____
....
_____
....
_____

What information does the picture give?

_____
....
_____
....
_____
....
_____

Ready-to-Use Independent Reading Management Kit: Grade 1   Scholastic Teaching Resources

☆ **Fiction 1 • Writing**

Name _____ Date _____

Book Title _____

Question and Answer

Write a question about your book.
Use a question mark. ?

_____
_____
_____
_____
_____

Write the answer to your question.
Use a period. .

_____
_____
_____
_____
_____
_____
_____
_____

Name _____ Date _____

Book Title _____

Syllable Sort

Find words in your book with one or two syllables.
Write a word in each box. Cut out the boxes.
Shuffle the cards and sort them by the number of syllables.

One-Syllable Words

Two-Syllable Words

Ready-to-Use Independent Reading Management Kit: Grade 1   Scholastic Teaching Resources

☆ **Fiction 1 • Skills**

Name _____ Date _____

Book Title _____

Short-*a* Poster

Find short-*a* words
in your book.
Write them on the
cat's poster.

Short-*a* Words	
cat	
nap	

Ready-to-Use Independent Reading Management Kit: Grade 1 Scholastic Teaching Resources

Name _____ Date _____

FICTION 2

Independent Reading Contract

Book Title _____

This book was (circle one):   easy   just right   hard

Complete the activities based on your book.
Mark each box after you have finished the activity.

Reading	Writing	Skills
(Choose ____)	(Choose ____)	(Choose ____)
Read to yourself.	**Who? What? Where?** Answer questions.	**What Did They Say?** Use quotation marks.
Read to a friend.	**Main Event** Draw a picture and write about it.	**Adjective Balloons** Find describing words.
Read _____ _____.	**Create a Cover** Draw a new book cover.	**Barnyard Vowels** Find short-*e* and long-*e* words.

Ready-to-Use Independent Reading Management Kit: Grade 1 Scholastic Teaching Resources

Name _____ Date _____

Book Title _____

Who? What? Where?

Be a reporter about your book.
Answer the questions below.

Who is the main character?
_____

_____

What is the book about?
_____

_____

_____

Where does the story take place?
_____

_____

_____

Ready-to-Use Independent Reading Management Kit: Grade 1   Scholastic Teaching Resources

Name _____ Date _____

Book Title _____

Main Event

Draw a picture of the main event in the story.
Write a sentence about it.

_____

- -

_____

- -

_____

Ready-to-Use Independent Reading Management Kit: Grade 1 Scholastic Teaching Resources

Fiction 2 • Writing

Name _____ Date _____

Book Title _____

Create a Cover

Draw a new cover for your book.
Write a sentence about it.

Name _____ Date _____

Book Title _____

What Did They Say?

What did the characters say in your book?
Write two sentences that the characters
said or might say.
Put quotation marks around them.
Write the characters' names.

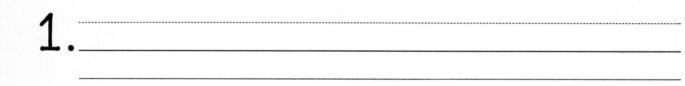

Example

"I love to fly!" —Bonnie Bird

1. _____

_____

_____

2. _____

_____

_____

Ready-to-Use Independent Reading Management Kit: Grade 1   Scholastic Teaching Resources

Fiction 2 • Skills

Book Title _____

Adjective Balloons

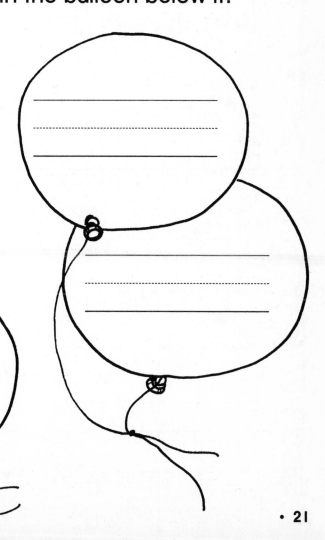

red

balloon

Adjectives describe people, places, animals, and things.
Find three adjectives in your book.

Write an adjective in each of the top balloons.
Write the word it describes in the balloon below it.

Name _____   Date _____

Book Title _____

Barnyard Vowels

Look for short-*e* words in your book.
Write them in the hen's pen.

Look for long-*e* words.
Write them in the sheep's pen.

Short *e*

Long *e*

Ready-to-Use Independent Reading Management Kit: Grade 1   Scholastic Teaching Resources

Fiction 2 • Skills

Name _____ Date _____

FICTION 3

Independent Reading Contract

Book Title _____

This book was (circle one):   easy   just right   hard

Complete the activities based on your book.
Mark each box after you have finished the activity.

Reading	Writing	Skills
(Choose ____)	**(Choose ____)**	**(Choose ____)**
Read to yourself.	**Plot Train** Write about 3 events.	**Word Soup** Find names of people and places.
Read to a friend.	**Up, Up, and Away!** Describe the main character.	**Sight Word Search** Look for sight words.
Read _____ _____ _____ .	**Picture This!** Draw a setting.	**Action!** Find action words.

Ready-to-Use Independent Reading Management Kit: Grade 1   Scholastic Teaching Resources

Name _____

Date _____

Book Title _____

Plot Train

Choose three events from your book.
Write a sentence about each.

What happened first?

What happened next?

What happened last?

Fiction 3 • Writing

Ready-to-Use Independent Reading Management Kit: Grade 1   Scholastic Teaching Resources

Name _____ Date _____

Book Title _____

Up, Up, and Away!

Draw the
main character
in the basket.
Write words
about the
character
on the lines.

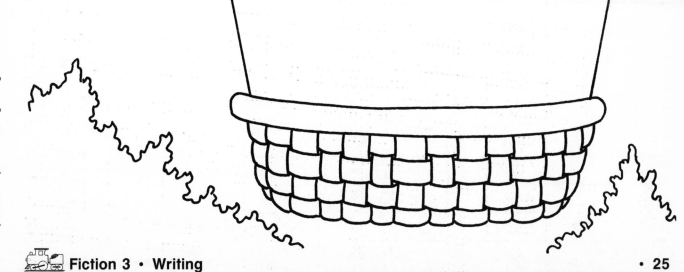

Name _____ Date _____

Book Title _____

Picture This!

Choose a setting in your book. Draw a picture of it on the easel. Write a sentence about the place.

_____

_____

_____

_____

Ready-to-Use Independent Reading Management Kit: Grade 1   Scholastic Teaching Resources

Name _____ Date _____

Book Title _____

Word Soup

The names of people and places always begin with capital letters.

Find names of people and places in your book. Write these words in the bowl.

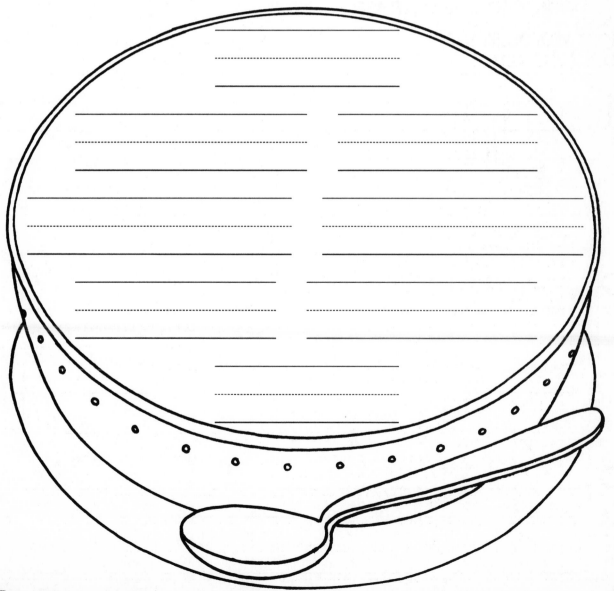

Ready-to-Use Independent Reading Management Kit: Grade 1   Scholastic Teaching Resources

Name _____ Date _____

Book Title _____

Sight Word Search

Read the words in the box.
Then look for these words
in your book.
Copy three sentences from
the book with any of these
sight words in them.

Sight Words				
it	did	the	not	there
is	and	said	was	where

1. _____

   _____

   _____

2. _____

   _____

   _____

3. _____

   _____

   _____

Ready-to-Use Independent Reading Management Kit: Grade 1   Scholastic Teaching Resources

Fiction 3 • Skills

Name _____ Date _____

Book Title _____

Action!

Look in your book for words
that show action.
Write each word in a shoe.

Examples
jump
sing

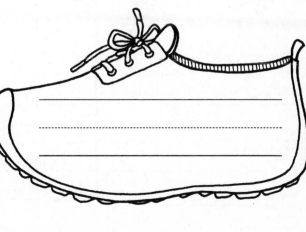

Name _____   Date _____

FICTION 4

Independent Reading Contract

Book Title _____

This book was (circle one):   easy   just right   hard

Complete the activities based on your book.
Mark each box after you have finished the activity.

Reading	Writing	Skills
(Choose ____)	(Choose ____)	(Choose ____)
Read to yourself.	**Library List** Choose books for a character.	**Treasure Chest** List the characters' treasures.
Read to a friend.	**Favorite Part** Draw a picture and write about your favorite part.	**ABC Order** Put words in ABC order.
Read _____ _____ _____ .	**Setting Chart** Compare two places.	**Short-*i* Fish** Find short-*i* words.

Ready-to-Use Independent Reading Management Kit: Grade 1   Scholastic Teaching Resources

Fiction 4

Name _____

Date _____

Book Title _____

Library List

List three books the main character would enjoy.

Tell why the character would like each one.

Name of Main Character: _____

Book Title	Why the Character Would Enjoy It

Name _____ Date _____

Book Title _____

Favorite Part

What was your favorite part
of your book?
Draw a picture of it.
Write a sentence telling why you liked this part.

```



```

_____

- -

_____

- -

_____

Fiction 4 • Writing

Ready-to-Use Independent Reading Management Kit: Grade 1   Scholastic Teaching Resources

Name _____ Date _____

Book Title _____

Setting Chart

Choose a setting in your book. Compare it to a place you have visited. In the chart, write three things about each place.

Place in the Book:	Place You Have Visited:
1.	1.
2.	2.
3.	3.

Book Title _____

Treasure Chest

On the left, write a character's name + **'s.**
On the right, write something the character owns.
Choose things that are important to the characters.

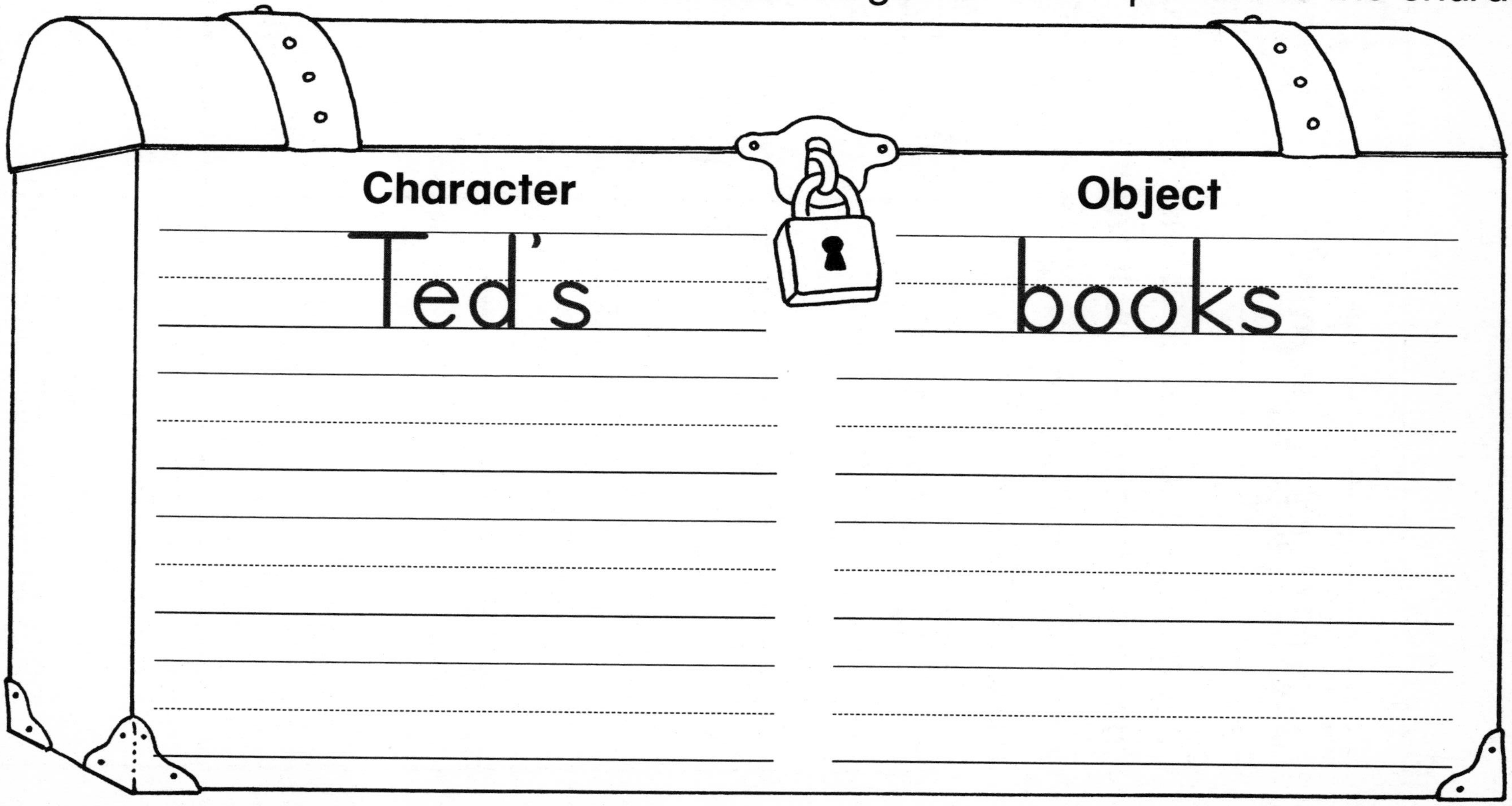

Character

Ted's

Object

books

Ready-to-Use Independent Reading Management Kit: Grade 1   Scholastic Teaching Resources

Fiction 4 • Skills

Name _____ Date _____

Book Title _____

ABC Order

Find six words in your book that start with different letters.
Write one of the words in each apple.
Cut out the apples.
Put the words in ABC order.

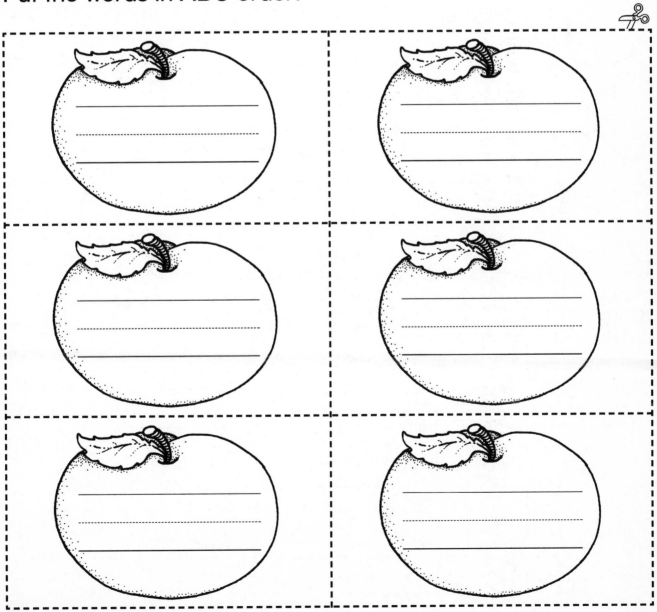

Fiction 4 • Skills

Name _____   Date _____

Book Title _____

Short-*i* Fish

Examples
swim
fin

Find short-*i* words
in your book.
Write a word in each fish.

Ready-to-Use Independent Reading Management Kit: Grade 1   Scholastic Teaching Resources

Fiction 4 • Skills

Name _____   Date _____

FICTION 5

Independent Reading Contract

Book Title _____

This book was (circle one):   easy   just right   hard

Complete the activities based on your book.
Mark each box after you have finished the activity.

Reading	Writing	Skills
(Choose ____)	**(Choose ____)**	**(Choose ____)**
Read to yourself.	**Character Chart** Compare yourself to a character.	**Word Boat** Find contractions.
Read to a friend.	**Problem Solved!** Write about the problem and solution.	**Sentence Scramble** Put a sentence in order.
Read _____ _____ _____ .	**Book Award** Give your book an award.	**Dog and Bone** Find short-*o* and long-*o* words.

Ready-to-Use Independent Reading Management Kit: Grade 1 Scholastic Teaching Resources

Name _____ Date _____

Book Title _____

Character Chart

Choose a character in your book.
Compare yourself to the character.
In the chart, write three things about
yourself and the character.

My Name:	Character's Name:
1.	1.
2.	2.
3.	3.

Ready-to-Use Independent Reading Management Kit: Grade 1   Scholastic Teaching Resources

Name _____ Date _____

Book Title _____

Problem Solved!

Describe the main problem
in your book.
Then tell how it was solved.

What was the problem?

_____
_____
_____
_____
_____
_____

How was it solved?

_____
_____
_____
_____
_____

Ready-to-Use Independent Reading Management Kit: Grade 1   Scholastic Teaching Resources

Name ______________________ Date ______________

Book Title ________________________________

Book Award

Examples
Best Characters
Best Ending
Best Pictures

Give your book an award.
Explain why it deserves the award.

Award:

____

____

This book wins the award because

____

____

____

____

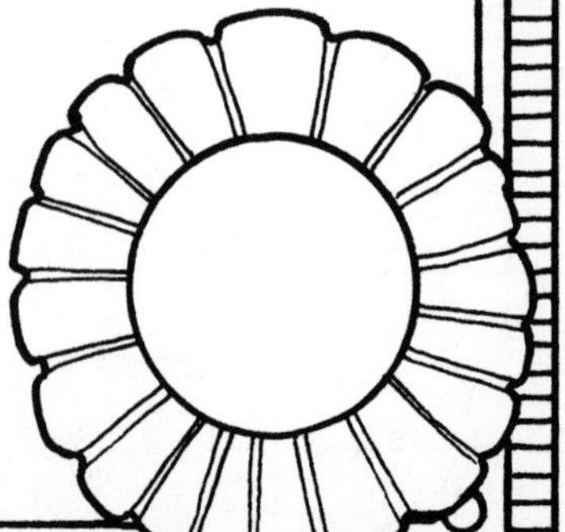

Ready-to-Use Independent Reading Management Kit: Grade 1 Scholastic Teaching Resources

Name _____   Date _____

Book Title _____

Word Boat

Find three contractions in your book.
Write them in the left sail.
What words make up each
contraction?
Write them in the right sail.

isn't

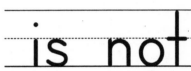

1. _____
2. _____
3. _____

1. _____
2. _____
3. _____

Ready-to-Use Independent Reading Management Kit: Grade 1   Scholastic Teaching Resources

Name _____ Date _____

Book Title _____

Sentence Scramble

Copy a sentence from your book.
Cut apart the words.
Put them back in order.
Then ask a friend to put them in order.

_____

_____

_____

_____

_____

_____

_____

_____

_____

Ready-to-Use Independent Reading Management Kit: Grade 1   Scholastic Teaching Resources

Name _____ Date _____

Book Title _____

Dog and Bone

Find short-*o* words
in your book.
Write each word in a dog.

Find long-*o* words.
Write each word in a bone.

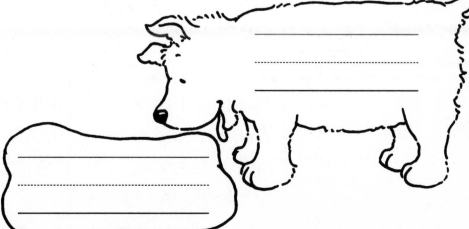

Ready-to-Use Independent Reading Management Kit: Grade 1   Scholastic Teaching Resources

Name _____ Date _____

NONFICTION 1

Independent Reading Contract

Book Title _____

This book was (circle one):   easy   just right   hard

Complete the activities based on your book.
Mark each box after you have finished the activity.

Reading	Writing	Skills
(Choose _____)	**(Choose _____)**	**(Choose _____)**
Read to yourself.	**Idea Flower** List the main idea and details.	**Great Sentences!** Write three types of sentences.
Read to a friend.	**Ask the Author** Write three questions for the author.	**Noun Search** Find nouns.
Read _____ _____ _____ .	**Take a Look** Write about a picture, chart, or diagram.	**Ducks in a Row** Find short-*u* words.

Nonfiction 1

Ready-to-Use Independent Reading Management Kit: Grade 1   Scholastic Teaching Resources

Name _____ Date _____

Book Title _____

Idea Flower

What was the main idea of your book?
Write it in the center of the flower.

What details support the main idea?
Write a detail in each petal.

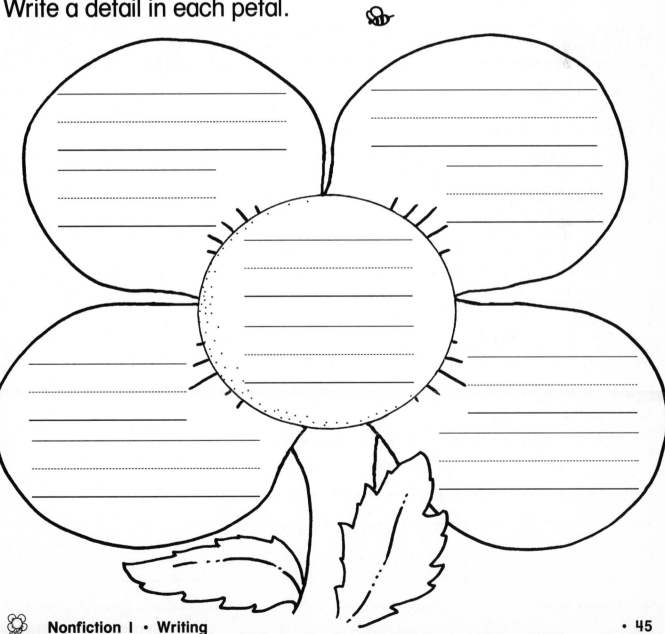

Ready-to-Use Independent Reading Management Kit: Grade 1   Scholastic Teaching Resources

Name _____ Date _____

Book Title _____

Ask the Author

What else would you like to know about the topic?
Write three questions for the author.

Question 1:

_____

- -

_____

- -

_____

Question 2:

_____

- -

_____

- -

_____

Question 3:

_____

- -

_____

- -

_____

Ready-to-Use Independent Reading Management Kit: Grade 1   Scholastic Teaching Resources

Name _____ Date _____

Book Title _____

Take a Look

Choose a picture, diagram, or chart from your book.

Describe what it looks like.

_____
_____
_____
_____
_____
_____
_____

Tell what you learned from it.

_____
_____
_____
_____
_____

Ready-to-Use Independent Reading Management Kit: Grade 1   Scholastic Teaching Resources

Name _____ Date _____

Book Title _____

Great Sentences!

Write a **telling sentence** about your book.
Use a period. $\boxed{.}$

_____
- -
_____
_____
- -
_____

Write a **question** about your book.
Use a question mark. $\boxed{?}$

_____
- -
_____
_____
- -
_____

Write an **exclamation** about your book.
Use an exclamation point. $\boxed{!}$

_____
- -
_____
_____
- -
_____

Ready-to-Use Independent Reading Management Kit: Grade 1   Scholastic Teaching Resources

Nonfiction I • Skills

Name _____

Date _____

Book Title _____

Noun Search

Nouns name people, animals, places, and things.
Find nouns in your book. Write them in the chart.

People or Animals	Places	Things
 girl bear	 forest	 chair

Name _____ Date _____

Book Title _____

Ducks in a Row

Find short-*u* words in your book.
Write a word in each duck.
Then cut out the ducks and
put them in ABC order.

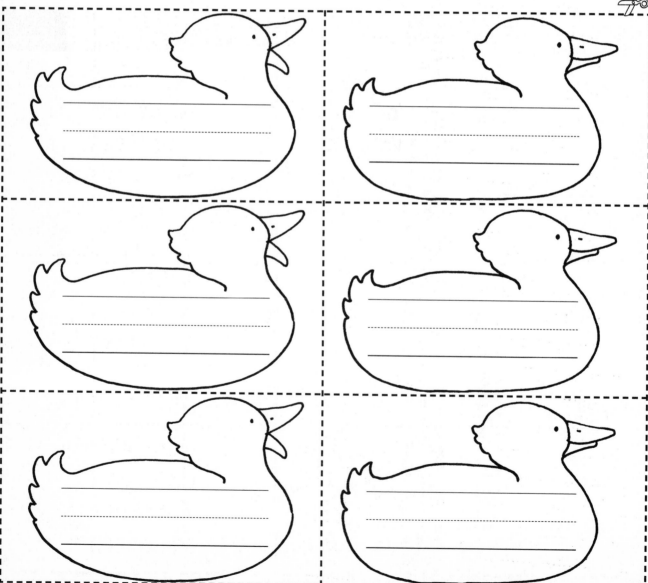

Nonfiction I • Skills

Ready-to-Use Independent Reading Management Kit: Grade 1 Scholastic Teaching Resources

Name _____ Date _____

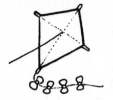

NONFICTION 2

Independent Reading Contract

Book Title _____

This book was (circle one):   easy   just right   hard

Complete the activities based on your book.
Mark each box after you have finished the activity.

Reading	Writing	Skills
(Choose ____)	**(Choose ____)**	**(Choose ____)**
Read to yourself.	**Fact Kites** Write facts from your book.	**What Do You See?** Use commas in a list.
Read to a friend.	**Be an Explorer!** Write about places in your book.	**Title Time** Write two new titles.
Read _____ _____ .	**Follow the Footprints** Write three events in order.	**New Words** Use new words in sentences.

Name _____ Date _____

Book Title _____

Fact Kites

A fact is something that is true.
Find three facts in your book.
Write a fact in each kite.

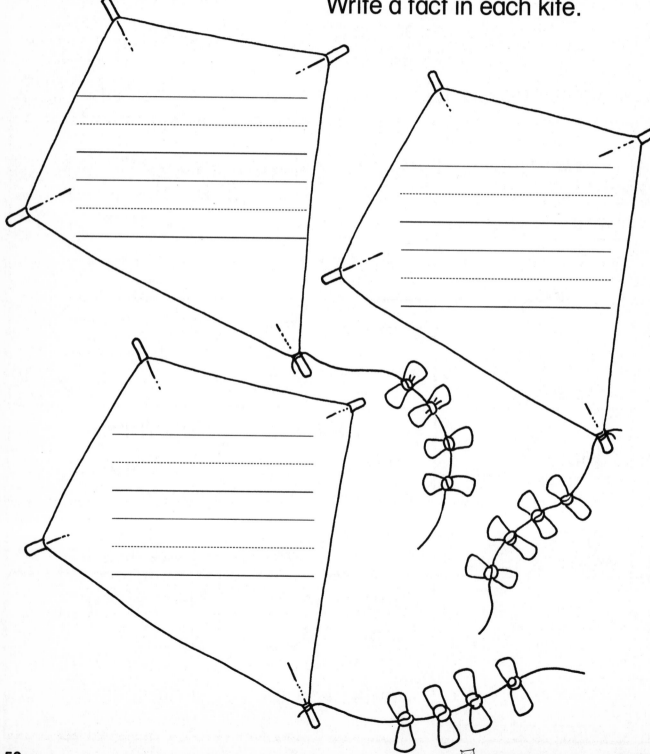

Ready-to-Use Independent Reading Management Kit: Grade 1   Scholastic Teaching Resources

Name _____ Date _____

Book Title _____

Be an Explorer!

Imagine you have visited the places in your book.
Choose your two favorite places.
Write a sentence about each.

Favorite Places

Place 1: _____
_____
_____
_____
_____

Place 2: _____
_____
_____
_____
_____

Ready-to-Use Independent Reading Management Kit: Grade 1 Scholastic Teaching Resources

Name _____

Date _____

Follow the Footprints

Book Title _____

Choose three events in your book.
Write each event in a footprint.
Write them in the order they
happened.

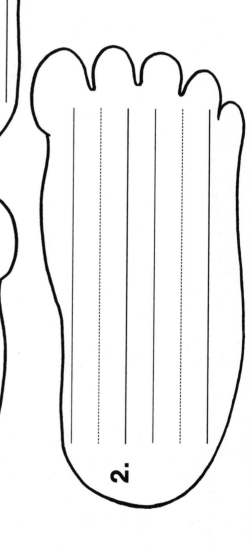

1.

2.

3.

Ready-to-Use Independent Reading Management Kit: Grade 1 Scholastic Teaching Resources

Nonfiction 2 • Writing

Name _____

Date _____

Book Title _____

What Do You See?

Choose two pictures in your book.

List three things that you see in each picture.

Use commas to separate the words in each list.

Example

I see a monkey, a banana, and a tree.

Picture 1

I see _____

Picture 2

I see _____

Name _____ Date _____

Book Title _____

Title Time

Important words in a title
are capitalized.

Write two new titles for your book.
Capitalize the first word, the last
word, and important words.

1. _____
   _____
   _____

2. _____
   _____
   _____

Ready-to-Use Independent Reading Management Kit: Grade 1 Scholastic Teaching Resources

Nonfiction 2 • Skills

Name _____ Date _____

Book Title _____

New Words

Find three new words in your book.
Write your own sentence with each word.

Word   **Sentence**

_____   _____
------------------   ------------------------------
_____   _____

                            _____

                            _____

_____   _____
------------------   ------------------------------
_____   _____

                            _____

                            _____

_____   _____
------------------   ------------------------------
_____   _____

                            _____

                            _____

Ready-to-Use Independent Reading Management Kit: Grade 1   Scholastic Teaching Resources

Name _____ Date _____

NONFICTION 3

Independent Reading Contract

Book Title _____

This book was (circle one):   easy   just right   hard

Complete the activities based on your book.
Mark each box after you have finished the activity.

Reading	Writing	Skills
(Choose ____)	**(Choose ____)**	**(Choose ____)**
Read to yourself.	**People and Places** Make a list.	**Rainbow Words** Write words that have the same meaning.
Read to a friend.	**True or False?** Write true and false statements.	**What Do They Do?** Write sentences about your book.
Read _____ _____.	**Most Interesting Part** Draw a picture and write about it.	**Nice Mice** Find words with long and short vowels. **a e i o u**

Ready-to-Use Independent Reading Management Kit: Grade 1   Scholastic Teaching Resources

Nonfiction 3

Name _____ Date _____

Book Title _____

People and Places

Who did you meet in your book?
List the people (or animals) you
read about.

_____

_____

_____

_____

_____

_____

_____

What places did you read about?
List the places in your book.

_____

_____

_____

_____

_____

_____

Ready-to-Use Independent Reading Management Kit: Grade 1   Scholastic Teaching Resources

Name _____ Date _____

Book Title _____

True or False?

What did you learn from your book?
Write two things that are true.
Make up two things that are false.

True

1. _____
   _____
   _____
   _____

2. _____
   _____
   _____

False

1. _____
   _____
   _____
   _____

2. _____
   _____
   _____

Ready-to-Use Independent Reading Management Kit: Grade 1   Scholastic Teaching Resources

Nonfiction 3 • Writing

Name _____ Date _____

Book Title _____

Most Interesting Part

Draw a picture of the most
interesting part of your book.
Write a sentence about it.

_____

- -

_____

- -

_____

Name _____ Date _____

Book Title _____

Rainbow Words

Find three words
in your book.
Think of words with
the same meaning.
Write the word pairs
in the clouds.

Nonfiction 3 • Skills

Ready-to-Use Independent Reading Management Kit: Grade 1   Scholastic Teaching Resources

Name _____

Date _____

Book Title _____

What Do They Do?

Choose three people or animals in your book.
Write a sentence that tells what each one does.

Person or Animal	What Does It Do?
A spider	spins webs.

Name _____ Date _____

Book Title _____

Nice Mice

Find words with short and long vowel sounds in your book.

Write the long-vowel words in the long-tailed mouse.

Write the short-vowel words in the short-tailed mouse.

Ready-to-Use Independent Reading Management Kit: Grade 1 Scholastic Teaching Resources

Nonfiction 3 • Skills

Name _____ Date _____

NONFICTION 4

Independent Reading Contract

Book Title _____

This book was (circle one):   easy   just right   hard

Complete the activities based on your book.
Mark each box after you have finished the activity.

Reading	Writing	Skills
(Choose ____)	**(Choose ____)**	**(Choose ____)**
Read to yourself.	**Time to Retell** Use your own words.	**Alphabet Search** Find words that begin with each letter.
Read to a friend.	**In the Picture** Write captions for pictures.	**Adjective Chart** Write adjectives and nouns.
Read _____ _____ .	**Blast Off!** Make a list of details.	**Word Frogs** Look up new words.

Ready-to-Use Independent Reading Management Kit: Grade 1   Scholastic Teaching Resources

Date _____

Book Title _____

Time to Retell

Choose a page from your book.
Retell the information in your own words.
Draw a picture.

Page _____

Nonfiction 4 • Writing

Ready-to-Use Independent Reading Management Kit: Grade 1 Scholastic Teaching Resources

Name _____ Date _____

Book Title _____

In the Picture

A caption tells what is in a picture.
Find two pictures in your book.
Write the page numbers.
Write your own caption for each picture.

Picture 1   Page _____

Caption:

_____

- -

_____

- -

_____

Picture 2   Page _____

Caption:

_____

- -

_____

- -

_____

Ready-to-Use Independent Reading Management Kit: Grade 1   Scholastic Teaching Resources

Name _____ Date _____

Book Title _____

Blast Off!

Find a description
in your book.
What does it describe?
Write it at the top
of the spaceship.
Write a detail in each
of the other parts.

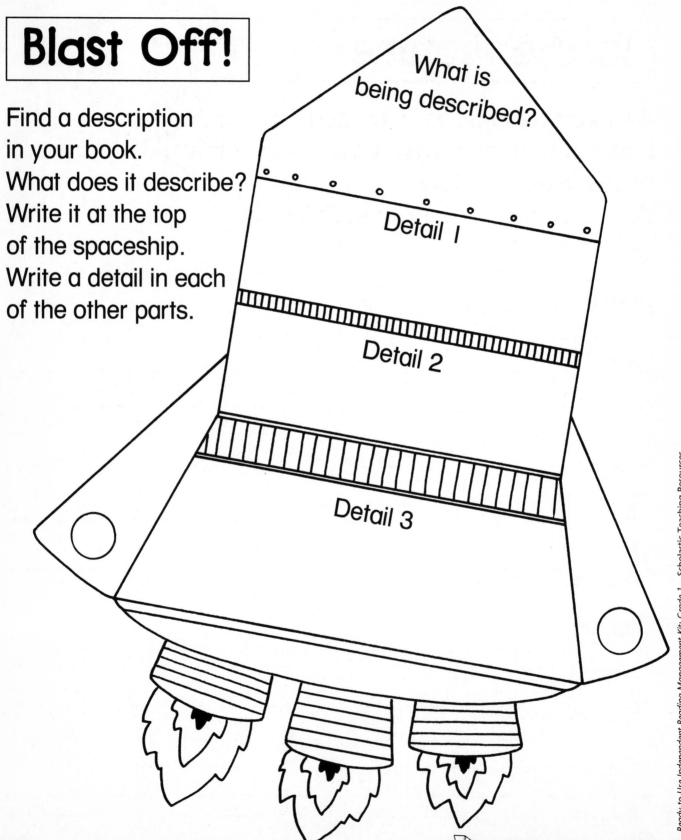

What is
being described?

Detail 1

Detail 2

Detail 3

Ready-to-Use Independent Reading Management Kit: Grade 1   Scholastic Teaching Resources

Nonfiction 4 • Writing

Book Title _____

Alphabet Search

Find words in your book that begin with each letter.
If you can't find a word for each letter, think of one instead.

A _____   N _____

B _____   O _____

C _____   P _____

D _____   Q _____

E _____   R _____

F _____   S _____

G _____   T _____

H _____   U _____

I _____   V _____

J _____   W _____

K _____   X _____

L _____   Y _____

M _____   Z _____

Name _____ Date _____

Book Title _____

Adjective Chart

Nouns name people, animals, places, or things. Adjectives describe nouns. Choose three nouns in your book. Write an adjective that describes each noun.

Adjective	Noun
playful	kitten

Ready-to-Use Independent Reading Management Kit: Grade 1 Scholastic Teaching Resources

Name _____ Date _____

Book Title _____

Word Frogs

Find four new words in your book.
Write a word in each frog.
Cut out the frogs.
Write the meanings on the back.

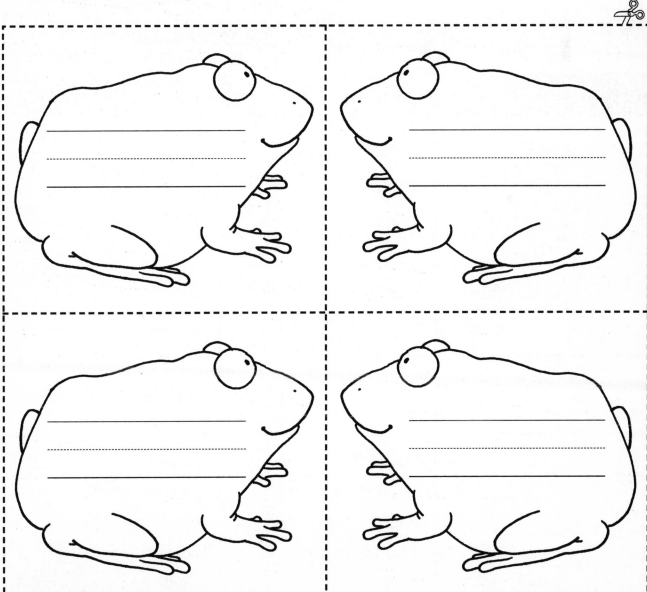

Name _____ Date _____

NONFICTION 5

Independent Reading Contract

Book Title _____

This book was (circle one):   easy   just right   hard

Complete the activities based on your book.
Mark each box after you have finished the activity.

Reading	Writing	Skills
(Choose ____)	(Choose ____)	(Choose ____)
Read to yourself.	**Send a Postcard** Write about a place.	**Book Reviews** Review your book.
Read to a friend.	**Butterfly Chart** Write facts and opinions.	**Old Sock, New Sock** Write pairs of opposites.
Read _____ _____.	**Lots of Learning!** Write about what you learned.	**Super Sentences** Copy sentences from your book.

Ready-to-Use Independent Reading Management Kit: Grade 1   Scholastic Teaching Resources

Name _____ Date _____

Book Title _____

Send a Postcard

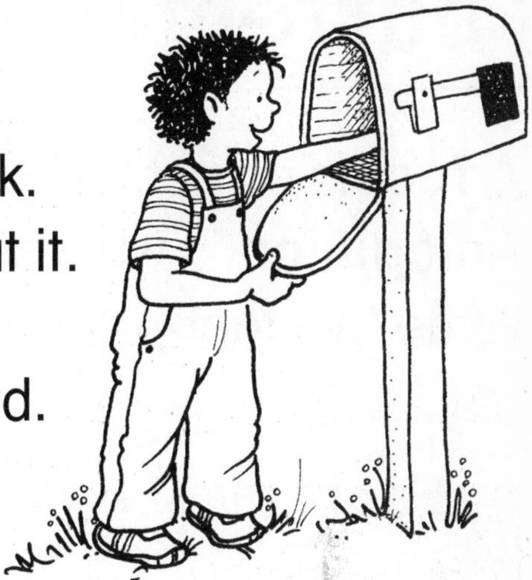

Choose an interesting place in your book. On the left, write what you learned about it. On the right, address the postcard to someone you know. Cut out the postcard. Draw a picture of the place on the back.

Name _____ Date _____

Book Title _____

Butterfly Chart

A **fact** is something that is true.
An **opinion** is what someone thinks.
Write two facts and two opinions about your book.

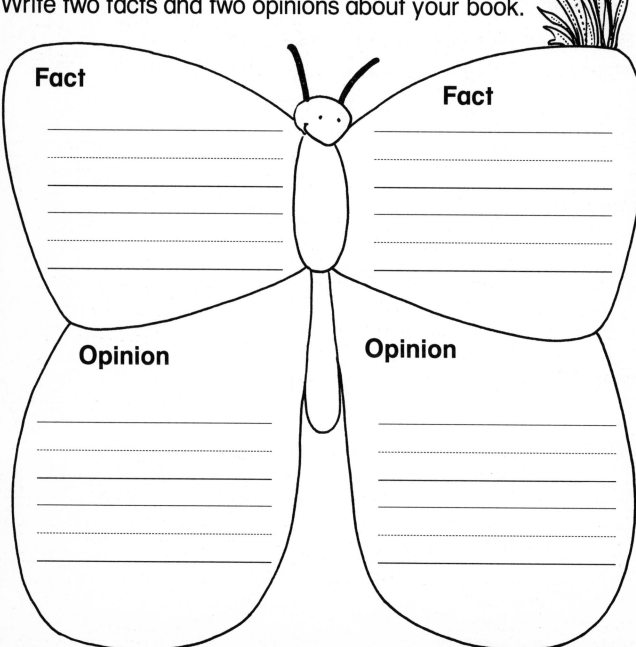

Fact
_____
_____
_____
_____

Fact
_____
_____
_____
_____

Opinion
_____
_____
_____
_____

Opinion
_____
_____
_____
_____

Ready-to-Use Independent Reading Management Kit: Grade 1   Scholastic Teaching Resources

Nonfiction 5 • Writing

Name _____ Date _____

Book Title _____

Lots of Learning!

My book is about _____.

What did you know about the topic
before reading your book?

_____

_____

What did you learn about this topic
from your book?

_____

_____

What do you still want to know
about this topic?

_____

_____

_____

Ready-to-Use Independent Reading Management Kit: Grade 1   Scholastic Teaching Resources

Name _____   Date _____

Book Title _____

Book Reviews

Make up two creatures to review your book.
Write a sentence that each creature might say about it.
Use quotation marks.
Draw your creatures on the back of this page.

Example

"This book is filled with interesting
information about the ocean."
—Wally the Walrus

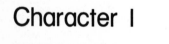

Character 1

_____

_____

_____

_____

Character 2

_____

_____

_____

_____

Ready-to-Use Independent Reading Management Kit: Grade 1   Scholastic Teaching Resources

Ready-to-Use Independent Reading Management Kit: Grade 1   Scholastic Teaching Resources

Name _____

Date _____

Book Title _____

Old Sock, New Sock

Find three words in your book.
Think of a word that means
the opposite of each.
Write the word pairs in the socks.

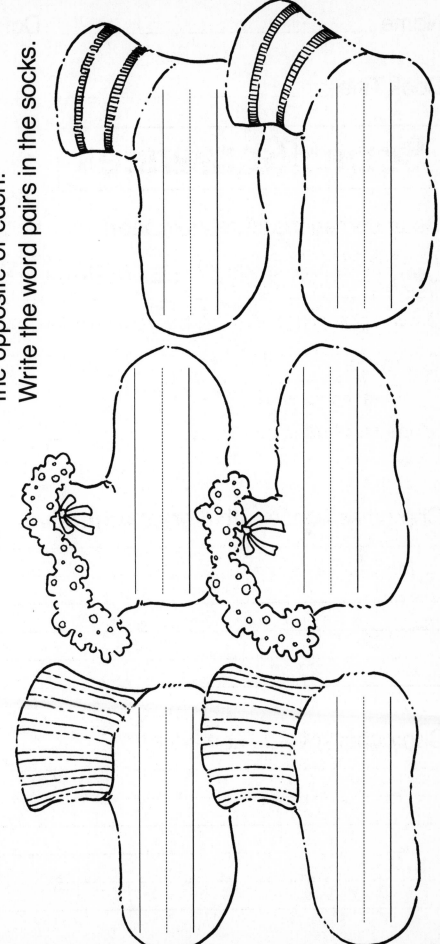

Name _____ Date _____

Book Title _____

Super Sentences

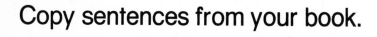

Copy sentences from your book.

Copy a sentence with a great **action verb**.

_____
_____
_____
_____
_____

Copy a sentence with a great **adjective**.

_____
_____
_____
_____
_____

Copy your favorite sentence.

_____
_____
_____
_____
_____

Ready-to-Use Independent Reading Management Kit: Grade 1   Scholastic Teaching Resources

Letter Home

Dear _____,

   Throughout the year, the students in my class will be reading books of their own choice. To help children get the most out of their books, our reading program features independent reading contracts. Each contract offers a variety of activities that encourage students to respond to fiction and nonfiction in meaningful ways. The activities build skills in reading comprehension, writing, vocabulary, grammar, punctuation, phonics, and more. Children make choices about which activities they will complete. On some contracts, they will be given the choice to read to someone at home. I hope that you will enjoy helping your child fulfill this important part of the assignment.

   When children are ready, we will move on to another contract that reinforces new skills. Before we begin a new contract, I will teach the skills necessary to complete it. Children will meet with me after they have finished a contract to talk about both the book they read and the activities they completed.

   In addition to building important language arts skills, independent reading contracts help children learn to work independently and purposefully. Although there is a wide variety of activities in the contracts, the structure and procedures are consistent. This allows children to work on their own while I am meeting with individuals or small groups.

   The goal of our independent reading program is to foster a love of reading and to help children build important reading and writing skills. I look forward to helping each student reach this goal. Please feel free to call me if you have questions.

   Sincerely,

   _____

Name _____ Date _____

Independent Reading Contract

Book Title _____

This book was (circle one): **easy** **just right** **hard**

Complete the activities based on your book.
Mark each box after you have finished the activity.

Reading (Choose ____)	Writing (Choose ____)	Skills (Choose ____)
Read to yourself. 		
Read to a friend. 		
Read _____ _____ _____.		

Ready-to-Use Independent Reading Management Kit: Grade 1 Scholastic Teaching Resources